"It has always seemed strange to me",
said Doc.

"The things we admire in men,
kindness and generosity, openness, honesty,
understanding and feeling
are the concomitants of failure in our system.

And those traits we detest,
sharpness, greed, acquisitiveness, meanness, egotism
and self-interest are the traits of success.

And while men admire the quality of the first,
they love the produce of the second.

—John Steinbeck

This
compendium
is in loving
memory of

LORRAINE & JOSEPH BEGNER

two people
who nurtured
and cared for
my darling—
the lady I adore,
who has been
my wife,
my idol,
my lover,
my friend.

ACKNOWLEDGEMENTS

Marjory Payne

educator, baker, mother, and friend,

who graciously shared

her vast knowledge and love

of poetry with

a struggling

seat-of-the-pants poet.

Jack Slutzky

artist, teacher, father, and friend

who inspired me

so many times

while producing this collection.

It's Poetry: Suck it Up!

Reflective moments in life

G.S. GOODMAN

*Nature is
a recurring theme,
partly because
I make
frequent trips
to LeRoy, NY
when frustrations
call for
emergency counsel
from my friend
Jack
and his
no-holds-barred
reality.*

FIELDS

The uncompromising plow
advances stubbornly,
crunching the clotted soil,
coughing up
huge clumps of clutter,
leaving lush, rich,
arable farmland
in its wake.

Amid the misshapen shards
of cornstalks, fresh
green stubble has emerged
to colonize the field
in interminable numbers,
progeny of the
previous Fall harvest.

Solemn patriarchal oaks
hover mute and protective,
gesticulating upon
whispers of temperate air,
swaying hypnotically,
and summoning me
onward.

*When I was
a boy,
I spent most of
my days
in solitary exploration
of Fairmount Park
in Philadelphia.*

*I thank God
for allowing me
a childhood
in which
fear was
not a player.*

*It was
during these excursions
that I became
a keen observer
of nature
and felt
compelled to draw
the beauty
my eyes
beheld every day.*

WINTER'S END

The winds abandon turbulence,
in exchange for
graceful morning breezes
that skip nimbly
over the listless landscape.

At first light
rowdy sparrow divas
join a chorus of raspy blackbirds
to proclaim disgruntled contempt
for the passing scene.

Meticulously,
Mother Earth labors
to stimulate
burgeoning life
across the dreary countryside.

Grunge and grime,
drab remnants of
a bleak winter,
dissolve after imprisoning
the terrain for many months.

Newly spawned gnats
gyrate in zigzag pirouettes
as they frenetically frolic
in life-affirming
dances.

And inevitably,
the majority of the populace
slogs on,
blissfully ignorant of
the reawakening.

Entrenched in
common apathy,
humankind vacillates
inevitably between insensibility
and animal instinct.

SUNSHINE

*The joke in
Rochester, NY is,
"If you don't like
the weather–
wait a few minutes".*

*The weather
can change
from one minute
to the next.*

*We soon learn
to give thanks for
every smidgeon
of sunlight.*

Heated air expands,
rises, and envelops
my consciousness,
warms my essence,
and reforms my spirit into
a delicate mist
which floats ever higher,
heavenward–
to mingle with other
languorous
bits of detritus
which have accumulated
in God's
celestial repository.

WINTER JEWELS

*In western New York
there are
ample opportunities
to sit and look at
falling snow
whitewashing
the landscape,
and creating
an immaculate,
shimmering
Wonderland*

*When our daughter
became a teen,
I wrote poems
for her,
to try to
reconnect
and diminish
her anger.*

Battling frost
and chilling winds
that whip snow into
gaudy trinkets
of ersatz jewelry,
a bent female figure
fights relentlessly
against frigid fingers
intent on
snatching away solace.

At Last!
Sanctuary. Home.

She scampers
inside her snug refuge
and is greeted by
brilliant purple
and yellow smiles
radiating from a cluster
of phenomenally
flawless flowers.

Jen, herself
imparts warmth
and brilliance
into lackluster moments.
Her extraordinary
and uncompromising principles
reveal her as
a steadfast legacy
her mother and I
will leave behind.

WINTRY SHADOWS

I look forward to,
and welcome
snow-covered
landscapes
during the
holiday season—
a white Christmas
with all it's
Bing Crosby
promises.

Sleet rakes the glass,
etching zig-zag patterns
on slick surfaces
frosted by arctic gusts.

Temperatures plummet.
Nothing moves
within the frigid stillness
of the out-of-doors.

Life is at a standstill.
Frozen in time.
Bereft of warmth
and animation.

Darkness settles in
softening edges,
and concealing
form and mass.

The inky curtain drops,
obliterating ambiguity,
leaving only the sovereignty
of my inviolate lodgings,
to define
the tangible world.

SOME OTHER MOTHER

*The sweetest
person
in the world was
my mother-in-law.*

*She never
raised her voice,
or uttered
an angry word.*

*If she had a fault,
it would be
that she trusted
that God
would resolve
all dilemmas.*

Propped there,
she awaits,
the translucent husk
of a woman.
Once proud,
and straight,
and strong.
Now,
limp and immobilized.
The burden of frailty
has transformed her
into a miniature
of the remarkable
teacher, mother, and
grandmother
her prominent days
once celebrated.

SWEET LORRAINE

*Lorraine Begner
was the
only real mother
I've ever known,
and she was just
a dozen years
older
than me.*

*I smile
at my most
treasured memory
of her.
When we would leave
I'd kiss her
and say,
"goodbye old woman",
and she'd smirk
and respond,,
"goodbye old man."*

Hello old woman,
remember me?
I'm from the life
that used-to be.

You mothered us
with constant joy,
grandmothered Jen
and brother Joey.

We yearn so
for the mom of old,
relentless drive
and love untold.

You pass your days
in silence bound,
your world's within
the world around.

You've no regrets;
accept God's will,
your temporal home's
a bitter pill.

Divine trust,
the bond you honed
for eighty years
with God, alone.

You cling to life
for what it's worth,
to spend more time
with us on Earth.

Our spirits flag,
oh, how we'll miss,
this glorious mom,
when gone to bliss.

NIGHTDREAMS

Flimsy flakes tumble languidly
in inexhaustible supply.
Without—the heavens are
peppered with heavenly gossamer,
erratic shimmering shavings
in the ebon sky
replicating themselves
in mirror-like collaboration;
time-honored envoys
of Christmas Eve conviviality.

Phantom nattering
floods the house
with the titter of children
from bygone years.
Gifts, long since lost or broken,
miraculously reappear
beneath the tree,
as rollicking specters
reenact the excitement
of past yuletides.

Then reality returns
and these cherished apparitions
disband and dissolve.
Gramma and Grampa look on,
unobtrusively abandoning the reins
to Jen and Joe,
who affectionately
initiate their children
into our dearly loved
family rituals.

*I miss
the times
when our kids
were small
and eager
for Christmas.*

*Their absolute faith
confirmed the reality
of Santa Claus!*

*Laughter,
torn wrappings,
holiday
food smells,
and delighted shouts
infused
the house
with infinite joy.*

FUNNY

Geese are silly creatures.

*Ponds are part of
the ambiance
at Marketplace Mall
in Henrietta, NY.*

*Geese have invaded,
and taken up
permanent residence,
living large, as if
they paid the rent.*

*State law dictates,
and humanity
insists that
these feathered clowns
are afforded
right of way.*

They affect a natty appearance
as they waddle forth,
oblivious to
potential hazards
posed by pedestrians
and lurching vehicles–

assuming implicit immortality,

which is a totally
delusional state of mind
for an avian
with a brain
the size of
a huckleberry.

16

EVENTIDE

*We live in
an unforgiving
climate
that presents us with
as much as
one hundred fifty
inches
of snow from
October to May.*

*This gives
a whole new meaning
to the phrase:
"Winter Wonderland"*

Snowflakes spin idly
in random patterns,
disturbing celestial luminosity
as they flicker and flare
in the evening's compliant,
lustrous firmament.

Indoors,
twinkling multicolored lights
peek furtively
in unabashed imitation
of the cosmos,
from the sanctuary
of a nurturing evergreen.

A lone angel
stands watch
above a contingent
of figurines and forms
that dangle unashamedly
amid reflective orbs
and glittering garlands;
myriad reflections
translated into
rich feral hues.

It's Christmas Eve,
With enchantment.

Silently
we survey–
delighting in
winter's wonders.

NOSTALGIA

*I remember
how joyous
holidays were
when all the family
was housed under
one roof.*

*This year is difficult,
Harriet's Dave
is gone,
Aunt Orva,
and Norene's mom.
The kids are living
elsewhere,
Joe in NYC and
Jen in
Brighton, NY.*

*The house is quiet,
except for the cats,
and they
aren't
party animals.*

Christmas morn was once the time
when tots and Santa reigned sublime,
essential players of the day
midst dazzling boxes, bright and gay
inspired squeals of household fun,
our blessings reckoned one-by-one.

Each of us, content within
this yuletide season we begin,
the cheerfulness of eager voices,
at each unwrap, a child rejoices.
A pine tree clad in shiny globes
the Christmas poem, and other odes.

Amidst this fuss– delighted wiggles,
Parental smirks and small-fry giggles.
An ideal bond 'tween young and old,
as jolly legends are retold,
To bed at last, so Nick can come,
deliver toys, and hurry on.
So sleeping moppets will be thrilled
to wake and find their stockings filled.

Our fascination for it all–
impatient kids, who wake to call:
Mom! Dad! Get up– it's Christmas day!
And we must rouse without delay.
We love this precious brood for sure,
on Christmas day, adore them more.
No finer calling can be had,
Than being someone's mom or dad.

JENNIFER
IN WINTER

*Our daughter
has been
a source of
both
joy and pain.*

*We've had
difficulties
in our relationship
but prefer to
remember only
positive
occasions.*

*Fantasies
are satisfiying,
mainly because
theyyoften
improves with age.*

She faces
the lethal Arctic winds
that forge
ribbons of snow
into razor-sharp blades
able to penetrate
vulnerable flesh.

Treacherous legions
assault all comers,
sweeping over
the crusted crests of ice
to obstruct pathways
and lay siege
to all survivors.

She stumbles inside
into the presence of
one, faultless,
blood red rose–
standing grandiloquent
in its crystal citadel,
a survivor of
these egregious,
grueling conditions.

Another beauty.
Her new best friend.
An unmitigated
soulmate during these
challenging struggles
with the unrelenting
wrath of winter.

MARCIA

*Our friend
was diagnosed
with cervical cancer.
on't worry,
she says.*

*You'd have to
meet Marcia
to understand
her approach to life.*

*Her health problems
are life-threatening,
but she chooses
to live every day
as if absolutely
nothing is wrong.*

*If you hear
loud tee, hee, hees
across the room,
that's bound to be
our Marcia!*

She titters
as she discloses
she has cancer.

But, not to worry,
everything will be okay.
Because she knows
it will be gone
after the operation.

Her heart
will withstand
the stress of surgery,
so we shouldn't
be concerned.

Damn her!!!

But,
thank God
she was right!

RAIN

I love rain.

*Since childhood
I've been fascinated
by raindrops
in puddles,
wind-driven droplets
across
the surface of
lakes or oceans,
rivulets running down
window panes.*

*There is a serenity
conveyed,
as well as
vivid memories
of the dry
aftershave fragrance
of rain
on hot sidewalks,
the salty taste of
drenching gusts
that blow in
off the ocean,
and the maritime smell
of salt-saturated
boardwalks.*

The air is dank
with cloying musk
which infuses
sodden surroundings
with oppressive
innuendo.

Ominous turbulence
disrupts nearby woodlands,
leaf-rustling bushes and trees
with furtive,
fitful gusts.

The sky's complexion
morphs to
mawkish green,
as billowing clouds
swell like bloated bubbles
and rise up
to obscure
the feckless firmament.

And then,
abruptly,
the clouds detonate!
and we are
doused
by pelting drops
of precipitation.

EPHEMERA

*As a child
I never understood
why my
value system
differed so much
from others.
My things
were super-special
to me.*

*As an adult,
my things are
just as precious,
but I am still
confused.*

Why is it
anything I prize
when viewed through
someone else's eyes,
is never valued
quite as much,
deemed worthless rubbish,
when nonesuch.

Misfortune reigns,
O'er missing things,
Beloved baubles—
kid's or king's.
Bereft as soon as
they are lost,
And can't replace
at any cost.

Dissuaders should
commiserate,
they could fall victim
to this fate—
some favored keepsake
takes a roll,
to vanish down
a rabbit hole.

So, should you see
a child upset,
sympathize with his regret,
a cherished item
once adored,
may have been
wrested from
his hoard.

PHILLY VISIT

*Our son
never wants
to lie to us,
so instead,
he avoids
telling us anything
that isn't
in our
best interests.*

Joe's in Philadelphia.
We think.
Playing with his buds
And holding hands with Melissa.
Love is an uplifting force,
But women are evil.
Just ask Joe.

MY PRAYER

I would prefer
it not be determined
that I passed this way
by the disorder
I left behind,
but by the beauty
I discovered
and left for all
to find.

*One day,
after being upset
by disarray in
Joe's bedroom,
I wrote this poem
which evolved
from a complaint
into a prayer.*

SILENCE

*Some people
love to
flap their gums.*

*Trivial conversation
for talking's sake
is one of the banes
of my existence.*

*If you don't
pay attention
it doesn't matter,
because they are
intent on
speaking their piece
regardless.*

Silence is
a benevolence,
which surrounds
and safeguards me
from the crashing waves
of insipid intercourse
that break, burble
and eddy
at my feet,
eventually
to be
carried away
on the rising tide
of clarity.

GOODBYE CHARLIE

We love our cats

We've had cats since we were first married, beginning with rascally Ralph Meeker.

Buster and Charlie were brothers who came to us and made the the whole household smile.

Buster was killed in the road, leaving brother Charlie. And then...

Fraidy cat Charlie–
darted in front of a passing car
and broke my heart.
It didn't do him
much good either.

There's no puss
to sit on the black chair
and talk to me
as I assemble my lunch.

There's no one
to coax through the cat door.
Because,
there's no more Charlie!

HOWCUM

Life is so absurd.

Eagerness is squandered
on adolescents,
while prudence
is the
prime bailiwick
of the mature.

Young kids
have it right–
   play hard,
         make your own rules;
            and don't question!

If weather permits,
         go outside.

*Sometimes,
I feel moved
to point out
some of life's
incongruities.*

*Resolution is not
necessarily available,
so I indulge myself
in mixing metaphors.
And occasionally
produce something
verging on profundity.*

MEN'S GROUP

*For eight years
I was part of
a group of men that
met weekly
to explore maleness.*

*It was a forum
in which we could
seek understanding for
the differences
between
men and women,
our differences,
and how the sexes
could interact
more successfully.*

*The jury is
still out.*

We question
in ever-widening circles,
a mixed fellowship of professionals
seeking the deep-seated
underpinnings of masculinity,
while paying homage to
the merits of sensitivity.

Sum and substance,
complaints, tearful disclosures
tenderly met head-on
with patience,
fellowship, and understanding.

During this intense
inner scrutiny,
each of us
found, empirically–
that we did not live in cowardice,
but actively confronted
society's crashing waves,
while conformists
continued to cower cautiously
on the shore.

THE
TRUTH FAIRY

*As honest
and true
as an Eagle Scout.*

Religious.

*Demonstrated
devotion to
family and
his fellow man.*

*He moved up
the corporate ladder,
until one day
he objected to
an unprofessional
liason
in the office,
and subsequently
found himself
back in the stores.*

*Rank sets the
benchmark for
divine
dispensation.*

Honest Pat Guider,
had to speak his mind,
because he is a decent man
and believes that
everyone
should be that way.

So now
he's pushing product again;
putting in hard time,
awash in decency–
is honest,
ethical,
Pat Guider.

FATHER'S REFRAME

Pedantic behavior
is a set of well-worn steps
which lead to predictable results.
A course of action
which excludes
the interruption of
unanticipated, arbitrary variables.

Maybe!

There will be no surprises,
nothing unforeseen
to cope with.
Only anticipated outcomes,
each and every time.

Totally!

This explains the eccentric's
absorption in producing
repeatable results–
a strategy
shrewdly employed
for centuries
by educators and theologians.

Certainly!

*My daughter
is compulsive.
She operates in
unbroken cycles
of set activities,
eating familiar foods,
and adamantly
clinging to
long-standing patterns.*

*I started
this poem
as a denunciation
of anal-retentive people,
and then
came to realize
that there might be
an upside to it.*

IDEAS

*Where do
creative thoughts
come from?*

*Einstein said ,
"Creativity is
inspiration
based on experience".*

*I believe ideas
are the result of
the unconscious mind
arranging
disparate elements
into logical
combinations.*

Occasionally,
during periods
of prolonged introspection,
I hear words
    that have no voice,
and behold shapes
    that have no form.

Inspirations
are autonomous
childlike
    flights-of-fancy,
to which
I attribute
no conscious meaning.

    They are chimeras.

So, why do people insist
that diaphanous delusions
become more coherent?
    To what end?

I prefer to think
that dreams,
awake or sleeping,
are illusory
paranormal venues
in which our
subconscious
dissembles vagaries
    into fodder
to nourish our
imaginations
and focus awareness.

SLEEPLESS

No rest,
No pause,
No peace-of-mind,
Thoughts won't subside,
Slow down, or go away.
The dubious clock
Ticks off the tedium of time.
Unsympathetic
        and relentless,
As night creeps slowly on
Lacking leniency
        or relief.

*Joe and I
sat on the porch
drinking beer,
and feeling good.
We had our first
in-depth
discussion,
during which
he described to me
how he copes with
a brain that is
propelled by ADHD.*

*He can't sleep,
because his mind
won't stop processing.*

*I'm proud of
how he has reframed
his situation:
"It's okay, Pop,
sometimes it's hard,
but I've learned to
manage my ADD.
I recognize that
it's what
makes me who I am".*

*That's the attitude
of a real winner.*

NOSTALGIA

*Eric Porter is
a sphinx.
He is very
self-contained
and placid,
but can
speak volumes
with a minmum
of words.*

*He is the
Reader's Digest
version of the
human condition.*

*He is
an enigma.*

My friend
Eric Porter
and I were
roomies for a while
during the
break-up of
his marriage.

We existed
in parallel universes,
and only shared
a jar of peanut butter.

At the office,
he drank coffee continuously
and never
used the bathroom.

I thought that was
particularly odd.

FRIGHTENING

*After a visit
with Norene's
87 year-old
mother,
at St. John's
Nursing Home,
I began wondering
if the future
would
treat me kindly.*

*Could I
dodge the
infirmity bullet,
or would I be
subjected
to age-related
humiliation?*

I fear
it won't be overlong,
till time exacts its toll,
and I will sit
with mouth agape,
my wheelchair in the hall.

No puzzles,
jumbles, complex books,
will tax my inert eyes,
no visitors,
no tasty meals
too weak to even rise.

My kids will live
lives they deserve
with energy and vigor.
and I, forgotten–
left alone,
will grow small,
instead of bigger.

The days of grace,
once lost to me–
have made me cede the right,
to pick and chose
the things I want,
instead, take what I might.

This living death
is what remains
after fruitful years of toil,
I'll waste away
until the day
I'm added to the soil.

*My ego
was sagging
and I was
feeling old.*

*Jen and Joe
are gone,
grown,
and off on
their own
adventures.*

*Aging
does not offer
much in the way
of challenges
or rewards—
mostly
trials and
tribulations.*

MOVING ON

I've become a cheerleader
for the Goodman team this year,
Norene has taken over
while I bring up the rear.

Jen is nearby–to the West,
at Hilton Middle School
a savvy first year cornerback
que hablas Espanol.

Joe, the tight-end of the squad
as everybody knows,
is working hard at Mansfield U
with vigor and repose.

And I, the aging athlete,
stand by with pride and tears
to think that I once led this team
for over twenty years.

So, I'm put out to pasture,
which I'm assured I well deserve,
but still I long for action,
that required skill and verve.

Because of me, the team was formed
I taught them all the plays,
Now I'm banished to the sidelines
With the ghosts of yesterdays.

35

*For years
I yearned for
a lithograph
by a local artist,
but was too cheap
to part with
the money.*

*In 2002
we attended the
Memorial Art Gallery's
Clothesline Exhibit
and there he was
right up front.*

*I couldn't resist,
and we purchased
a Fall landscape.
I derive
immeasurable
pleasure
every time I look
at that scene.*

*It is a window
to another
time.*

It's magic.

TREES

A magic window on my wall
transports me to a time in Fall,
when vibrant visions I recall,
were etched in me, when I was small.

Dry, crackling leaves surround the park,
the cutting air, so crisp and stark,
disturbing echoes make me hark
to early days that left a mark.

Amidst this innate natural splendor,
my naive schemes and youthful candor,
I struggled to locate the door
that virtue led me to before.

Through introspection I may see
the decency inside of me,
then Judgment Day could prove to be
my doorway to Eternity.

A co-worker,
showed me
a moving article
his wife had written
about their stricken son,
published in
a major Rochester
newspaper.

I couldn't get it
out of my head,
and thankfully,
the story ends well.

It nits close to home
for every parent.
Yet, there must be
thousands of
similar stories
we never hear about,
just as touching,
but perhaps,
with fewer happy
endings.

PARADISE RECLAIMED

I read a wistful story today,
written by a grief-stricken mother
who was told her darling baby-boy
was born with a ventricular septal defect–

A hole in his heart.

Lucas would not make it
through the winter
without critical open-heart surgery.
His doting parents
were paralyzed with dispair
at the prospect that
they could live out their days
without their precious son.

The surgeon perfomed
a miraculous repair,
and Lucas would mend completely.
His first Christmas was spent
in the hospital, recovering,
but surrounded by family–
aunts, uncles, grandparents,
and mom and dad.

His cardiologist says he's fine now.
He's home with his grateful family,
and this year Christmas will be
a typical celebration.

Probably testing his parents' patience
like any normal two-year old.

SCHEMA

*Manliness
is perceived
differently
by each of us.*

*I define a real man
as one
who exhibits confidence
in his masculinity,
and accepts responsiblity
for his actions,
whether it be
blame or praise.*

What is the measure of a man?
How much he earns?
Attention span?

Is having money a big part?
Buys real estate?
Or priceless art?

What qualities will best portray,
The ideal male
We know today?

A multi-tasker, who's quite able
To run a business?
Build a table?

Hardworking or street smart,
Do certain traits
Set him apart?

Dynamic and good looking?
Body type?
Loves gourmet cooking?

Writes, fabricates, or draws?
Creative skills,
That reap applause?

Cynics argue and berate
Defining maleness
Through debate.

In the end, I'm prone to say
Most ideal men
Have feet of clay.

ICY COMMUTE

*Winter is
cold
and white,
in Upstate
New York.
The best
one can do
is learn to
appreciate
Jack Frost's
handiwork
as an
artform.*

If we can put aside
the inconvenience of
scraping off
the murky haze of frost
obscuring the windshield,
reducing our vehicles to
opaque sarcophaguses,
we would
rapidly discover that
the frigid temperatures
which crept in last night
fashioned an
enchanted fantasy world
festooned with
bizarre biscuit trees,
situated atop
undulating tiers
of white milk chocolate
and dusted with a glistening
sugar glaze.

CHILDHOOD'S LOSS

*What became
of my army of
tin soldiers,
Lone Ranger
secret decoder ring,
or
Jack Armstrong
bombsight?*

*Have you ever been
curious at how easily
the things we
cherished as children
simply disappeared?*

*They weren't lost
or thrown away,
they merely ceased
to exist.*

Whatever became
of my little brass sword
which stirred boyish delight,
with immaculate shine,
six inches of steel—
I loved to call mine.

I imagined I'd lead
cav'lry charges and such
with this venerable weapon
which on top all else lay,
chosen more often
than other items
of play.

I could be a pirate–
purloin booty and swag,
my scabbard tucked tightly
in a sash at my waist
protected by angels,
vanquish villains I faced.

Affection was lavished
on all of my toys
my room was my castle,
I shut reality out,
so I could control
what my life was about.

And now as I rue
that a token so dear
could go senselessly missing,
an undeniable truth,
abjectly I yearn for
things valued in youth.

Now I am grown
and succumbed to life's game,
like other adults
denied honors or joy
I yearn for the pleasures
once brought by a toy.

THE FARM

Cohocton, NY
is home to
rich farmland,
and
good friends
who retired there.

Judy's father
willed his farm to her
and she absolutely
adores it.
She keeps horses,
a cat, and a dog
and loves to play
farmer's daughter.

We descend
the meandering highway
that snakes its way
through Bristol Mountain,
in eager pursuit
of rest and revitalization–
destination: Naples, NY.

We cross the floor
of an enormous basin
embroidered with brilliant orange,
red, and yellow flowers,
embellishing hillside and
meadow alike.
The colors are too intense
to be believable.

The most skillful colorists
would be at a loss
to produce paint or dye
to match the brilliance
that Mother Nature
is able to infuse
into the countryside
with her autumnal palette.

Steep slopes rise on all sides,
swathed in finery
which extends to infinity.
As we crest the rise,
we are greeted by the final vista
of kaleidoscopic images
before we descend.

We suddenly peak–
then plummet towards the lake
through charming Naples,
past Canandaigua Winery,
to the turn for Cohocton,
a left and up again,
mounting the hills
which lovingly cradle
Hal and Judy's bliss--
Trails End Farm.

HALLOWE'EN

*When our kids
were young,
we'd follow
our little
costumed pretenders
as they moved
through the
neighborhood
begging candy.
"Trick or treat!"*

*When the night
was over
we'd gather
in the kitchen
and dump the loot
on the table.*

*Joe would wolf down
his stash
in a few days,
then beg Jen
for some of hers.
She hoarded her candy.
In fact I'll bet
she still has some.*

It's All Hallow's Eve
and the neighborhood
bustles with
elusive, stealthy figures
brandishing ludicrously
grizzled expressions,
menacing,
but hardly dangerous.
They feign intent to maim–
quintessential rogues
reminiscent of 1940s
B-grade horror films.

Blanketed in gloom,
this spectacle of
incessantly babbling,
multicolored goblins
pursues its rhythmic route
of coercive efforts
to convert
tricks into treats.

Burdened with
swollen bundles of booty,
they jabber in raucous voices
and unintelligible tongues,
tacitly agreeing
not to return
for another twelvemonth.

IMMACULATE CONCESSION

*Puns—
placing
the wrong word
in the right place
is my idea
of funny.
Ergo this title.*

*Puns drive Jen nuts,
like nails
on a blackboard,
and she always
corrects me.
One reason
I continue to
use them
is because
she's suckered-in
every time.*

*Also,
describing rain
with sexual
overtones
intrigued me.*

Raindrops splatter
soundlessly
against the unyielding glass,
deploying brigades
of spermatozoon militia
charged with
the vital mission of
inseminating Mother Nature.

They tap softly,
gingerly,
to announce their presence,
and welcome or not,
go about their task
like illicit smugglers
furtively transferring
contraband.

Their sworn objective
is to revitalize the earth
and replenish
the dwindling
aquifer.

Scrupulously,
the earth is purged
of accumulated detritus
and decay,
leaving it cleansed,
and ready to embark on
a new season.

DIRT ROAD

*Every two years
seniors should
have a colonoscopy
to protect
against cancer.*

*At age sixty-eight
I'd never had one,
and with the
boldness of health
I made an appointment.*

*When the time came
for the procedure,
I became a bit unsettled.*

*Not unlike the feeling
when you're stopped
by the police,
sure you did
nothing wrong,
but still expect
to get nailed.*

Peekaboo colon's
The game for today,
Won't breathe till it's over–
What the doctor will say.

Am I healthy inside,
Are there polyps about?
The big C's a question?
Of course, without doubt.

My diet consists
Of things liquid of sorts
Broth, Coke, orange jello
Black coffee, of course.

Drank a gallon of cleanser
To clean out my gut,
So I'm spotlessly clean
For those checking my butt.

The position assumed
Is distasteful at best,
For surveying my back door
In this odious test

What might be found
Is the worrisome part,
Perhaps diseased tissue,
I hope, a mere fart.

I wait for assurance
From the doc or his aide–
"No need for concern",
Then my qualms are allayed.

And right after that
I'll start to lose weight
To get into shape
For our next scheduled date.

GOLDEN RULE

*Traveling the hills
and dales
of Bristol, NY,
we experience
the magnificence
that is so
characteristic of
Upstate New York.*

God's country.

*Warm weather
tends to draw us
towards Naples
for the
Grape Festival,
a tasting
at local wineries,
or a pleasant visit
with friends
in nearby Cohocton.*

Daylight diminishes
and declines,
burnishing foliage with
rich orange-gold
highlights.

The bucolic landscape
blazes with iridescent grandeur
that flickers and shines
as though
a heavenly hand
had snatched chunks
of the Milky Way
and dappled
the hillsides with stars.

Delicate deposits
of dazzle
form an opulent quilt,
concealing
the ramshackle milieu
that's surrendered its color
dreary and
at cross-purposes
with the
bronzing patina
of Indian Summer.

IN AMERICA

*My daughter and I
used to
spend Sundays
together
during the
football season.*

*She had
an excellent
grasp of the game
and its intricacies,
and we'd
hoot and holler
at the teams.*

Sundays are for football,
Thrills and chills suffuse the air,
Frantic fans flock to their gridirons,
Simply manic to be there.
Pigskin pirates start parading,
Teams ferocious for a win,
Punish each other harshly
For a sewn-up piggy skin.

Braving frigid, wintry weather,
They're not to be denied,
Us? We're snuggled in our afghans
Keeping toasty warm– inside.
We view the game on teevee
Quite adequate for me,
Football's called a game of inches
Ours! Forty-six diag'nally.

Grunts and groans and horrid thuds
Wild fans cry and exhort
Like the Roman Coliseum
They lust for blood, not sport.
And when the day is over
Players hobbled and mayhemed,
The home team's play applauded,
And the visitor's condemned.

Whate'er the score, win big or lose,
Diversion is complete,
If after all that sitting
We can struggle to our feet.
Alas, the games are over!
What will we do for fun?
We have to wait another week
For new contests to be run.

Yes, football is quite brutal,
Brawny challengers contend,
The weekdays serve as buffers
That allow the teams to mend.
Next weekend we start all over
And quickly take our seats,
To view the new hostilities–
Tally vic'tries and defeats.

THERESA
AT THE GATE

For 5 years
I had lunch
once a week
at China Gate
Restaurant.

Two years ago
the owners retired
and sold to
Theresa and San Lee,
who continue to offer
a comparable menu,
but
lavished more
attention
on customers.

I know a classy lady,
A friend of mine you see,
Whose spirit and good breeding
Bespeak of royalty.

Serene in her demeanor,
A natural grace and wit,
Refinement, and gentility
Bear noble proof of it.

A rich and stately manner
Reflects a former time
When people were more gracious
Life, eternally sublime.

Her enigmatic smile,
And easy queenly grace,
Establishes a kingdom that
Transcends our time and space.

She brightens up the day
But, is modest and can't see,
The effects of the joy she brings
To commoners like me.

So patrons, let's be grateful
For this treasure we behold,
A kind and gentle head of state
Well worth her weight in gold.

LADIES LOVED

*I was
never too adept
at "guy" things. Just
couldn't play
the games.*

*I found
interacting
with the ladies
to be far
more interesting,
though I didn't
understand
them
much better.*

*Oh well,
at least
they smelled
good.*

Here's to ladies I have loved,
And later left behind.
Forever fixed within my heart
Both singly and combined.

Sweet phantoms of my early days
Now sealed in a domain
Where they will never wither,
They always stay the same.

They're as beautiful as ever.
They never seem to age.
I see them quite distinctly,
Like snapshots on a page.

With honeyed words and whispers
Captivating smiles and ways
Their girlish charms unblemished
As they were in olden days.

I cherish all these loves long gone,
Regret none, no surprise
Their presence in my early life
Did much to make me wise.

And so I pay great homage
To the sweethearts I did find,
Who continue to attend me
In the playhouse of my mind.

*Fear of death
is a futile
preoccupation.*

*The Grim Reaper
shows no favoritism
and will visit
each of us in time.*

*Continuing on
without loved ones
is not easy,
and it is my hope
that someone
will think of me
kindly from
time-to-time.*

MISS ME

In Springtime nature will call forth
lavish flowers, as usual.
redolent with ambrosial fragrance
   –when I am gone.

The sky will remain rich azure blue
with islands of cottonball clouds
   –when I am gone.

Winter's cold may deposit Jack's Frost,
but summer sun will offer restitution
   –when I am gone.

Spring once more will cloak
sullied surroundings
in garments of opalescent green
   –when I am gone.

Whispers of urgency will pass between
anguished lovers in ardent embrace
   –when I am gone.

The planet will continue to rotate,
and the seconds will skitter by
just as quickly as before
   –when I am gone.

Nothing will change significantly
in the next sweet installment of
life and living…

   *–except
    I will be gone.*

CHRISTMESS

*As a
devotee
of Christmas,
I am saddened by
the hypocrisy
evident
during the season.*

*The real
meaning of
Peace on Earth,
good will towards men,
has somehow
gotten lost amidst
the hustle and bustle
of gift giving,
gorging,
and partying.*

This time of year
is much awaited
but, peace and love
are over-rated.
Festive gifts
you get– no doubt
while those worse off
make do without.

I'm speaking to
cynics and putzes,
who question what
the whole damn fuss is.
Who consecrates
with trees and lights?
And then denies
folk's human rights?

To me it seems
unjustly skewed
that certain ethnic groups
get screwed.
Let's strike a blow,
starting this season–
no disrespect
for any reason.

We come into
this world the same,
but soon choose sides
to play the game.
Prejudice and
persecution
are thought by scores
an apt solution.

Life's not the same
for everyone,
but looking back–
what's done is done.
From here on out
be fair and strive
to show some class
while you're alive.

OIGA VAULT

*Making friends
is as easy as
a phone call.*

*I met Howard
on a
long distance call,
to repair
my wife's
engagement ring.*

*His voice echoes
of my past life,
when I was
surrounded
by Jewish culture.*

*That,
and the fact that
kindness is a trait
I have prized
in people
most of my life,
makes Howard
a venerable force
in society.*

Howard's silken tones
flow over and around me
in a flood of temperate air,
that reduces uncertainty
and alleviates apprehension.

I hear the smile
that colors his voice;
his words suggest
scholarly wisdom–
a somber rabbi
confering
in talmudic tones.

His personna is a
reflection of a society
whose tenets
have always been based in
gentility, honor,
and understanding.

The tumult
overshadowing
today's sense of obligation
is a sharp contrast to
kinder, gentler times,
now outmoded,
which he continues
to exemplify
with unfailing humility.

BUD

*My son lives in
New York City,
making his way
in the world
while seeking out
what he wants
to do
with the rest
of his life.*

*We don't speak
often,
and then
he's off-hand
or mumbles
vague responses.*

We don't do things together,
Or sit and chew the fat.
You don't know what I'm up to–
And I don't know where you're at.

You're a self-sufficient person,
Content to hold your own.
Keep your comings and your goings
In the realm of the unknown.

It would really, truly please me
If we could share a beer,
And you could fill me in on
The things I long to hear.

You've always been quite special
Made your mom and me so proud,
But you've never been a child
To discuss your life outloud.

Before my mind is vacant,
Before I pass away,
I pray that this will happen,
And I wonder what you'll say.

Joe's diploma
from Mansfield
came in the mail,
and it was
so attractive
I wanted to frame it,
but not without
his approval.

You see, I've learned
to stop making
decisions
for my adult son.

He's his own man,
and I want to
show him
the proper respect.

JUNE 11, 2003

It came by mail
For all to see,
Old Mansfield U.
Sent your degree.

It's more attractive
Than expected,
This sheepskin needs
A frame selected.

If that's all right
And you agree,
We'll bring it, framed
To NYC.

ROCK OF AGES

Eric is a stoic.
He's highly intelligent,
complex, indefinable,
and a complete
mystery
to me.

His wife Zola
probably
understands him.
I think he's
a puzzle.

But, at all times,
I am confident
of where I
stand with him.

For the
many things he is,
I love him.

The one thing in life
I can truly depend on,
is that Eric Porter
will remain constant forever.
He is like a colossal effigy
that has endured for centuries–
steadfast, fixed, and resolute.

In all likelihood,
he was forged when
relevant intensity,
combined with
congealed prudence,
to coalesce and consolidate
his primal being
into an infinite wellspring
of unshakable durability.

He is my rock.

APOLOGY

*Six months
and the pain of
her mother's death
still eats at
the core
of my lovely wife.*

*She misses her
every day,
and I miss her too.*

*We both cried at
Joe's graduation
from college,
because
Mother wanted
so desperately
to be there.*

*We'd like to
believe she was,
in some way.*

I'm sorry I'm unable
To take your pain away,
That I haven't been more thoughtful,
Planned a better Mother's Day.

I know your heart is heavy
And no matter what I do
I never can relieve that ache
That's deep inside of you.

A very special person died,
And left us all behind
The epitome of parent
Near impossible to find.

Time won't ever change things
She's as gone as gone can be
Continuing without her–
Inconceivable to me.

No matter how this day goes,
With regard to your misgiving,
One more day with your sweet Mother
Is the gift I would be giving.

I'm sorry that you hurt so
I wish I knew the ways
To help you through these tortured times–
Enrich your future days.

Alas, we're only mortal,
At the mercy of our fates,
We're precipitated onward
In pursuit of closing dates.

THE DEARBORN LEGACY

*Goodbye
dear friend.*

*Vale taught me
to be a good father,
to accept myself,
and to live life
to the fullest.*

*Norene and I
moved away
from Philadelphia
in 1975,
and that was the
last
we saw of her.
She returned to
Venice, CA,
resumed her
schooling
and became
a psychologist.
I checked in with her
twice a year,
through email.*

*Her last message
was devastating.
The cancer she had
fought continually
was about to
claim her.*

We met one starry evening
at a concert in the square
　　The group, I don't recall.

I took my place,
the very space
　　She claimed upon the wall.

Acceding to her righteous pride,
I parked beside
　　Beleaguered by lust's fires,

We talked, debated, fumed,
as fascination bloomed
　　Arousing raw desires.

When all was done,
she asked me home
　　But, I was faint of heart.

An anxious clown,
I turned her down
　　Her wedding ring, in part.

Next day, again we met,
Unsettled, still upset
　　Misgivings slightly melted.

We found the time was right,
made love all night,
　　Our bodies wet and welted.

Frenetic, non-conformist you
and me, the frightened mud-stuck Jew
　　Personalities quite unsuited.

Like fire and water never mix
we had conflicts,
　　And the passion was diluted.

The laughter and shared tears,
lightened up our fears
　　Dilemmas were deflated.

The best of her is part of me–
So sad that she will never see
　　Her knowledge inculcated.

Looking through
material
in my
storage file,
at work
I ran across
this untitled poem
written
some time earlier.

I was delighted
to know that
I had created
such a fine bit
of whimsy.

I felt
I had given myself
a present!

TIRED

My brain is full
Of much and more,
Packed cotton wool–
An apple core.

Don't crave a thrill,
No worthy tasks,
No tempting foods,
No vintage casks.

A bed would serve
To ease my load,
Just forty winks
Or I'll implode.

Can't force myself
To raise my head
To knuckle down,
Earn daily bread.

My weariness
May well be such
That standing up
Will prove too much.

Condemned,
I cannot satisfy
My need to rest
Until I die.

SIXTY-NINE

*We volunteered
at the
Mendon Arts
Festival,
and I worked
the dunking booth
for 3 1/2 hours,
in bright sun
without a hat,
bending
time and again
to pick up balls
and reset
the drop bar.*

*When I awoke
Sunday
I was in agony,
nursing a headache,
backache,
swollen hands,
and general
body trauma.*

When I awoke
Awash with pain,
To rise at all
Seemed quite insane.

To struggle up,
To stand and move,
To venture forth,
What would I prove?

Pain can't be detected
No one knows—
My abject gloom,
Who could suppose?

I won't complain,
I'll be abstruse
Resign myself
Beg no excuse.

At break of day
However slowed,
I must get up
And hit the road.

Can't disregard
My father's trait—
Show up for work,
And don't be late!

I ache to see
When I retire,
If I'll slow down,
Or just expire.

SMOULDERING

To some troubled souls
Life is an eternal conspiracy,
To be plotted, schemed
And implemented
With military precision.

Never surrender to intuition,
Stay dispassionate and detached.
When the prescribed moment arrives:
　　execute the plan,
　　forget any misgivings and
　　disregard queasiness.

With fury, they resolve
to remain steadfast in
the righteousness of their endeavor.
The clock proclaims the instant
of engagement,
and then comes
the frantic adrenaline surge.

When it's over,
unsettling misgivings linger,
because retribution
is deceivingly complicated,
and offers
no palatable resolution.

*Unhappy people
obsess over
ways to
wreak revenge
upon those they
believe
have placed
advantage
out of their reach.*

*They are petty,
discontented,
and insecure,
and consequently
are never comfortable
with their lot
in life.*

*When Joe comes,
to visit
we don't spend
much time together,
but It's nice
to at least
share meals
before we go
our separate ways.*

*He's off to
meet with old
friends,
and we
resume our
usual routine.*

VISITATION

Joe's returned,
A visit home,
We're glad he's here
So glad he's come.

Airport. baggage,
Borne away.
Some catch-up time,
Perhaps, today.

First off, we stop
To eat our fill,
The pasta place–
Romano's Grill.

A moth to flame
Ellen, who served,
Beguiled by Joe,
Was quite unnerved.

Top of his game,
Words dripping honey,
An urban wolf,
Who's oh so funny.

Genial, witty,
Handsome, and tall,
Forgets poor Ellen–
And makes a call.

Once home we chat
Five minutes or more,
Then quick as a shot
He's out the door.

We could complain
He doesn't relate
To boring old us,
Who're so out-of-date!

Nonetheless–
We adore our son,
But spend time with us?
Hell, we're no fun.

KADDISH

(Jewish lament)

A dear friend
died on
September 2, 2003.

We hadn't seen
each other
for 25 years,
but maintained contact
by phone and e-mail
for several years.

I was pleased
she answered
my last message.
That's when she
informed me
the doctors
had given her
two months to live.

There are
a handful of people
who had a
marked effect
on my life,
and she is
right at the top
of the list.

Vale ceased last Tuesday.
Unheralded.
While sleeping.

The Earth suffered no seismic calamity,
The sun supplied its usual
allotment of sunbeams and warmth.
And the birds continued warbling
their lovesongs with exuberance.

Meanwhile, in Venice, California
A soul crossed over.
A galvanizing spirit expired.
A glorious star relinquished its brilliance.

Vale Valentine was my dear friend!
As long as she was alive—
continued to exist in the world
and breathe air,
my equilibrium was secure.

The significance of this woman
will transcend separation.
Her clarifying insights,
and legendary exploits unearthed
the hesitant adolescent within me
and thrust him toward maturity.

A relationship
doesn't end because
someone dies.
Vale's inspiration and love
will continue to look after
this irrepressible Don Quixote
whom she always tried to dissuade
from battling windmills.

QUANDARY

As I get older,
aging is
a recurring theme
in my writings.

I'm continually
discovering
new twinges and quirks
that must be
catalogued,
quantified,
and explained.

I'm quite disappointed
that no one's
published
a user's manual
for people like me
to refer to.

The elderly are
plagued
with a physiology
reminiscent of
desert snakes.
Cool, ambient air
triggers
increasing sluggishness,
to the point that
they will desperately
seek refuge
in the nearest
available shelter.

But,
their dissimilarity
is most apparent
when you examine
who it is that
occupies
the warm rocks
of the desert,
and who
favors the
Early Bird Special
buffets.

SERIOUSLY

*Ocassionally
I am
inspired by
other writers
who lead
the way with
observations
quite similar
to what
I was
prepared to
convey.*

I go not willingly
into the night
but stand my ground
courageously–
long after suns
conclude their flight.

My rage proclaimed
in failing light
this crucial compact
duty-bound,
till all dissension
flees from sight.

Then, only then,
grim and contrite,
midst profuse
self-effacing tears,
I'll quit the fray
and say goodnight.

CATACLYSM

Our daughter
initiated
pain
in our lives
with intractable
stances
and conflicting
worldviews.

Sometimes
when I get weary,
the hurt
overwhelms me,
and my eyes
begin
playing tricks.

Exhausted,
weary beyond belief,
my eyes
follow images
cascading across
my computer screen,
when they are replaced by
a phantom visage
which assaults
my brain–
        eclipsing all else.

Blond.
Chic.
Clever.
        A most alluring smile.

Cherished offspring.
But callous.

The epitome of youthful vitality;
        our golden girl–
who has opted
to seek asylum
within
meaningless distraction.

THE LISTENING POST

*For several years
I have been
part of
the
Gates/Chili
Middle School
special
lunch program.*

*Adults
sit and talk
with 6th, 7th, or
8th
graders
and share their
lunch period.*

*Each session
includes a craft
that we
work-on together.*

*The kids tickle me,
but I still
don't understand
what they
get out of it.*

Who are you;
Who am I?
We meet for lunch–
I ponder why.
Since you are young
And I am old
Why should you care
What I behold?

When we sit down
We seem to work,
I'm not a kid,
You're not a jerk.
And as the days
Continue on
Our friendship swells
You're less withdrawn.

Too soon we see
Our time is done
You're on your way–
That ends the fun.
I fidget, wait
For time to pass
Till I'm assigned
Another class.

COMPUTER
BULL SHOOTER

*Some people
compulsively
tell lies.*

*I can't believe
they actually
think we are
gullible enough to
put our trust
in them.*

*One of them
was involved
in fixing my
laptop
computer.*

He'll have it ready Tuesday
Though he promised it today
Assured me for the past three months
Yet, still a week away!

I'm clearly disappointed
I want my laptop back
I don't foresee delivery
Till he has a guilt attack.

Chris can't adhere to deadlines
Though he truly means us well
Too often he gets sidetracked
And production goes to hell.

He has the best intentions
Will swear it's almost done
In an effort to appease us all
Quite often, pleases none.

He doesn't get his money,
I'm lacking my computer
The sorry lesson to be learned:
Don't put faith in a bull shooter.

NASH RAMBLE

Ogden Nash
had fun
writing poetry
on his own terms,
sometimes
making up words
and messing with
syntax.

I took it
a step further
and
made no sense
at all.

Excuse
the wombat and the gyre
Exuding
effervescent lyre
Gramorsed
with mandatory whey
Phrenolated,
day by day
Profusely
morphing shushy dum
Extrudes a
fetid, sloshy scrum
Midst
truculen banalus scant
Sore verbon
declamatious schrandt.

PISSED OFF

*We've all
experienced
the games
played
under the guise
of honesty,
humility,
and sincerity.*

*After
a while
I lose it!*

I'm not
doin'
this dance
anymore!

Can't. Won't!
It's over.
Done!

The promises.
The expectations.
The disappointments.

You revel in
your rude
and nasty games,

And I'll be damned
if I'm willing to play.

DELUSION

*A
reframe
for those
who rigidly
adhere to
misguided
conventional
thinking.*

Success
is achieved
by
governing
outcomes,
not by
restricting
options.

WEASEL WORDS

*How many
times
have we heard
phrases like,
"the check is
in the mail",
"I'll pay you back
Tuesday",
or
"I just need to
borrow this
for an hour"?*

*I've constructed
a
partial list
of these
empty words
and promises.*

Cross my heart and hope to die
Poke a sharp stick in my eye
Cross my fingers, cross my toes
Can't see a thing beyond my nose.

The gospel truth is what I've said.
May lightning strike me in the head
My hand to God, I give my word;
Me tell a lie? Why thay's absurd!

Oh yes, the check is in the mail
No such thing, an old wives tale!
I'll still respect you in the morn
I rue the day that I was born.

One good deed deserves another
He's not heavy, he's my brother
As busy as a two-bit whore
I've never felt this way before.

It's just a mid-life crisis thing
Tied to his mother's apron string.
But, after all is said and done
Half a loaf is better than none.

You can't get blood out of a stone
The lights are on, but no one's home
Wiser to let sleeping dogs lie
Or time will merely pass us by.

Promises, pledges, promotions, pacts
Are selective, wicked, impulsive acts.
These phony assurances, needless to say
Are merely deception grown into cliche.

JACK AND JILL
(The Adolescent Years)

*I continually
tease
my good
friend
Jack,
—because
I can.*

When Jack and Jill
went up the hill,
he pleaded that she orter.
But she was good,
"Like hell she would!"
Until he could support her

VIAGRA

A lampoon
of ED,
(erectile dysfunction).

Sometimes
there can be
differing
points of view
that make
me chuckle,
and I decided
to share
this one.

I once knew a man, name of Max
Restored by a teeny blue pill,
Engaged in lascivious acts
    Daily, and almost at will.

A virile and active bull terrier,
Revisits past masculine verve
His johnson's become a lot merrier
    It's willing and eager to serve.

Erections are instantly florid
Enhancing this gentleman's life.
Once flacid, now terribly torrid,
    To the utter dismay of his wife.

CAROL

*A swimmer
at the
Southeast YMCA
is a funny lady
who does part-time
nursing at Strong
Memorial Hospital.*

*She's
pretty outrageous
for a
professional,
but I suppose
that
makes her
all the more
interesting.*

Carol's not common, or fancy–
But a highly efficient Nurse Nancy

She's prone to play jokes
On all kinds of folks

Her guffaw's like
the cry of a banshee.

THE RAVIN'

Once upon a Tuesday dreary,
Fatigued, fahblunjided and weary
While nodding off or lightly napping
I roused to clamor – someone yapping
A yip yip yapping...never heard before.

Verbal bombast reached my hearing
Biting argot spewed– quite searing
Shouted in a New Yawk twang
A vile angrified harangue,
Insults...never ever heard before.

A pointy-nosed rapscallion
Who appeared to be mammalian
Raged and ranted, pitched a fuss
Boisterous as a blunderbuss
Inane drivel...much too often heard before.

This pretentious intercourse
Revealed no kindness or remorse
It was nowhere near beguiling
And, in fact, left no one smiling
Formed an anus...that wasn't there before.

Me, preoccupied with guessing
On what point he might be stressing
To an object of subservient misuse–
This mad tyrant's busted loose
Was unpleasant...a big bully, and a bore.

His intention though well-meaning
Was so forceful and demeaning
I would think he'd be most hated
But instead he's venerated
Commended...like I never saw before.

His goal was to inspire
And in the scheme of things – retire
Depression and unwarranted despair,
Constant critic of his peers
Out of teaching for twelve years
Super Jack, at last subdued...forevermore.

FIFTY-NINE
AND COUNTING

Another
birthday
poem.

I always
like to
find new ways
to keep
my cards
fresh and
interesting.

This birthday wish holds so much more
than Have a Happy Day.
Within my words lie lots of things
I never get to say.

Like, I adore you for your mind,
along with all you do.
You're fundamental to my life.
I'm awfully proud of you.

As a surprise, I'll tell you dear
for milestone fifty-nine,
to mark this added birthday year,
I've built a Norene shrine.

It's hidden in my secret heart
so only I can see
the woman, so exceptional—
you only share with me.

Happy Birthday!

I THINK OF YOU

A short note
to
my son
Joe.

Reassurance
that he is
thought of.

Every once in a while
you surface in my thoughts
and I wonder
what you're doing,
but then
I get caught up in
what I'm doing.

TWENTY-FIVE

*I'm proud
of Joe for
taking on NYC.*

*When I graduated,
I was afraid to
go to the big city.
So, I elected
to stay
in Philadelphia
and gave up
any chance
of being a mover
and shaker
in the
advertising biz.*

Happy birthday to Joe Good,
A quarter cent'ry, you've withstood.
Charmed by the Apple's siren voice,
Brooklyn's now your home of choice.

A former rural farmland feller
You morphed into an urban dweller
The ceaseless clamor, which I hear–
Is just sweet music to our ear,

You thrive upon big city ways
Undaunted by demanding days.
Your matchless talent can be seen
In programs on our TV screen.

THREE-SEASON ROOM

While staying
with friends
living next to
the Oatka Creek,
in LeRoy, NY,
I was captivated
by the
spectacular
daybreaks
that materialized
every morning.

I'm perched at the top the world,
in a majestic tree house
which towers
over Oatka Creek.
I preside over a vista
that rivals the majestic grandeur
of Tarzan of the Apes'
jungle escarpment.

No sound, no whisper,
no breeze.

Birds, every so often,
dart from branch to rooftop
and back again
in pursuit of some
gossamer delusions.

A slow moving ribbon
becomes a writhing band of color
which snakes its way
through the lush undergrowth,
and subtly delineates the far side
of the creek bed.

Flashes of dazzling light
pierce the emerald green canopy
revealing fragments of foliage,
then just as quickly withdraw,
restoring the status quo.

A sigh of tranquility.
A burble of sweet contentment.
God's tour de force beguiles
as daybreak continues to unfold.

ANNIVERSARY POME

*Every year
I write an
anniversary
poem
for my wife,
because
commercial cards
are never
personal enough.*

*They can't
describe
the intensity of
the relationship
we share.*

There comes a time
in simple rhyme
when moon
is paired with June,
or roses red
and violets blue
are all that can be said.

So, I despair
that such plain fare
can't tell how much
you've meant,
the diverse ways
you've filled my days
with loving complement.

For thirty years
you've calmed my fears
and been my heart's delight,
through smiles and tears–
diverse careers,
you loved me day and night.

In this reprise,
though now I wheeze,
my body's bent and broken,
this love endures,
is always yours,
I present this little token.

Our days were spent
without dissent
since you became post-bridal,
I love you most,
and proudly boast–
You'll always be my idol.

FIRST LIGHT

*The most
stunning view
of Oatka Creek
is early
in the morning,
at sunrise.*

*Watching
the panorama
take shape
in the shifting light
is kaleidoscopic.*

The creek stretches stark and still,
a dappled band of crystal
fractured now and again
by delicate strands of undergrowth.
Unintelligible forms
flit hither and yon
through the eerie miasma
that shrouds the
unfurling landscape.

In the midst of sheltering trees,
plants grope the loamy soil
for better purchase,
anticipating day will break
and they must secure their grip
on another day.

A sound distracts me,
and when I turn back
the canvas has changed
even further.
I am spellbound by
the sheer eloquence of
this primal manifestation
of unwavering continuity.

CHILI, NY
(pronounced ch-eye-lie)

*Our Mendon house
was on the market
for a year and a half
before it sold.*

*We found a
suitable replacement
but, the owners
asked a lot more
than
it was worth.*

*Our household goods
were in storage
and we were living in
Jack and Adriana's
basement.*

*After two weeks
we made another offer,
(for cash)
They countered,
we countered back.
They accepted.*

*Phew!
Home at last!*

We shifted
our life's journey
from the East side
to the other,
we've moved into a charming ranch
not far from Norene's brother.

Four minutes
are consumed,
to visit Ort and Pat,
ten minutes to the Geigers,
we can't improve on that.

Our neighbors
treat us kindly,
the house – completely suited
to me and my sweet honeybee
once homeless and uprooted!

Chili is labeled working class–
less status than in Mendon.
But, we prefer
these gracious folks
that seniors can depend on.

EVOLUTION RESOLUTION

*Why is it
necessary for
everyone to believe
that divine design
is the only
explanation for
the genesis of man?*

*An all-knowing God
is hard for me
to accept
on faith alone,
and yet,
I believe the human
body is
far too complicated
to have evolved
by chance.*

A kiss, a sneeze, a sigh,
procreation, healing,
eyesight, DNA,
passion, thinking,
affection...
are
arguable faculties
which indicate that
the complexities
of the human body
are too remarkable
to have ever
evolved from the
chance combination
of elements.

But,
if divine design
is argued
based on faith

where did God
come from?

JOE GOOD

*I dearly
love my son,
and every
once in a while
I think of him
with great
longing
and affection.*

*That's what
moved me
to write this.*

I'm
thinking of you,
as often I do,
with great pride
and a whole lotta
joy.

You're
a fine boychik whoish
the son of pop– Jewish,
and a mom
who was brought up
a goy.

This mixture of ethnics
aroused pyrotechnics
in the midst of
an obtuse
hoi polloi.

Now, quite successful
though sometimes
life's stressful;
you're renowned
as the
Goy Wonder Boy.

Oy!

THREE FOURTEEN

*In hospital
after
knee replacement
surgery,
I was suffering
a huge
amount of pain,
compounded by
bladder problems
and pretty sucky
meals.*

*How can
trained dieticians
prepare
some of the
worst food
imaginable?*

Bob Little's gone–
He surged my knee.
I'm shackled to
A bag of pee.
No bed for naps,
No tray to eat.
Two goofy socks
adorn my feet.

At last!
A vacant room is found
Where I can sleep
Or laze around.
As pain persists
From toe to hip–
My solace is
A morphine drip.

A liquid diet
Bobbie wrote,
No solid food
Will grace my throat.
The next day's fare–
Offensive stuff,
A bite or two's,
More than enough.

A three-day stay
And then I can
Indulge in meatloaf,
Cheese, or flan.
My taste buds
Are aghast at how
A cook would dare
To serve such chow.

Empty calories
Blanched and bland
A bill of fare
So clearly canned.
A tasty meal
Would sure be nice
Like egg fu young
Or pork fried rice!

CURMUDGEON

Damn them!
There's another bunch of
sniveling little brats
ringing the doorbell!
And I just sat down again.

Now I have to get up and
go to the door to
hand over more candy bribes
to three-foot high pirates,
astronauts, and ballerinas.

*Hope the sugar rots
their goddamn teeth.*

Don't parents have
anything better to do than
lead these little hooligans around
begging for handouts?

This dratted bag of candy cost me
over $10.00, dammit!

One bag better be enough
for these candy bandits
or I'm turning out the lights,
closing the drapes,
and hiding out in the bedroom!

*Sometimes
I behave
insensitively
when my body's
hurting and
overtired.*

*But, I
manage to
get over it and
join the fun.*

A CHILD'S VIEW
OF CURMUDGEONRY

My friend
and mentor said,
"Now tell
the same story
from the child's
perspective."

It was
a good exercise,
and helped me
apreciate
that disparities
exist between
points of view
in any story.

Who is that scary old man
who came to the door, growling,
and jammed candy in my hand?

*"Here's your treat, so no trick",
he snorts.*

He's the kinda man
I was told never to take candy from;
just run away screaming "help!"
Why would mom bring me to his house
and make me go to the door?
He slobbers,
and his look make me feel like
I'm a nasty bug.

I'll take his candy– to please mom,
but I'll throw it away.
It's probably poisoned.
I'm a little kid,
and he looks like
he wants to kill me.

Hurry mom!
Let's go to the next house.
Mrs. Denton lives there.
She's nice.

SIXTY-WAN

*A
birthday poem
for my
darling wife.*

*I can't imagine
having
finished my
reign on earth
without her
companionship.*

Aghast when you reached sixty,
You've added twelve months more
You struggle with discomforts
Unknown to you before.

Your eyesight is enfeebled
Body parts droop out of place
But, no real signs of aging
Appear upon your face.

I've loved you for forever,
You are my heart's ideal,
I imagined you before we met
And hoped that you'd be real.

You're all I've ever wanted
My life has been fulfilled.
Our devotion is unending
No one could be more thrilled.

So dear, a happy birthday
With many more to come
From a guy who's tres contented
By your side, my sweet Yum-Yum.

*Creativity
on-demand
becomes a
daunting task
occasionally.*

*Don't
get me wrong,
I love to do it,
but
inspiration
isn't
always
forthcoming.*

*Sometimes
I have to
stretch.*

MY VALENTINE

Each year I write a poem
and tell you of my love,
but you're aware, how much I care
and to the extent thereof.

I pledge to you devotion
today, next week, next year
and till my breath is taken,
I'll be loving you, my dear.

For lo, these many decades
I've proclaimed you my ideal,
you've made my life worth living,
and confirm our love is real.

You fill my life with sunbeams,
make me cheerful with your ways,
the pleasure of your company
vastly elevates my days.

With permission to continue
we'll live-on in harmony
I promise to adore you
and crowd your heart with glee.

MORNING

*Spinal stenosis
often causes
acute pain in
my back
and left hip.*

*Lying in bed
or sitting
I am pain-free,
so, I tend
to sit a lot,
and
take my time
getting out of bed
in the morning.*

I awake
to the rowdy assault
of the alarm clock,
but resist, roll over
and refuse to rise.

I burrow deeper into
my cozy pillow,
pull the covers tightly around me
and dissolve into sublime comfort.
My bed is my ecstasy.

Aaaaah!

Since this is the best
I expect to feel all day–
I tend to make the most of it.

The moment will come,
soon enough,
when I must
face the pain.

No need to
rush into it.

GOOD GRACIOUS GIRL

*My dear
friend Adriana
suffered a
stroke
just days before
her sixty-fifth
birthday party,
where I was
to present
this poem.*

Sixty-five!
and still alive,
after all
that you've
been through!

At times life was crazed
still, three children got raised
you managed
you coped–
and made-do.

Smitten with Jack
you never looked back;
scurried off
with the Jew
to make woo.

Your kids are all set
and yet you still fret–
want them happy
and joyful
like you.

Sit yourself back,
or cuddle with Jack;
chill-out
till your next
sculpture's due.

PAIN
PARADIGM

*Today
is a
hurting
day!*

Sheathed in
pulses of pain,

tethered to
limiting yokes,

ensnared by
circuitous chains,

beleaguered into
unsustainable stress,

deranged,
debilitated,
and demoralized–

I give way.

CONSTRUCTION

*A
nonsense poem
that
had its origin
while our house
was being
remodeled.*

Binga, wanga, blam.
Zum, zum.
>*Wham.*

Awga, bawga, bood.
>*Ping.*

Whappa, dappa, oop.
Buzzaw! Buzza
>*Bzzzzzzzzzzzzzz!*

Bling, bang, bong
Krumpa, sumpa, wong.
Ooga, nooga, zood.
>*Plang.*

Bzzzzzzzzzzzzzz!
Sagga, bagga, whump.
>*Whew!!!*

L u n c h !

Banga, danga, hud.
Kroota, doopa. dum
>*Bam.*

Ooga, wooga, zum, zum,
>Ding.

Whappa, zappa, tap, tap.
>*Yzzzzzzzzzzzzz!*

Whum, bam, jam-jam.
Krun, dum. umph.
Ooga, dooga, mooga,
>*Prang.*

Whippa, whappa,
Bza za za   za   zzzzz
>*W h o a!*

**Quittin' time!
Seeya t'morra.**

KEEPSAKE

*On my drive to
the YMCA,
I became aware
of
the lingering
presence
of my wife's
goodbye kiss.*

She kissed me
this morning
as she left
for work.

It was
a significant
improvement
to my lips.

The taste
of her lip-gloss
endured for hours,
along with
the delicious awareness
of belonging.

Each time
my tongue
explored my mouth,
I was delighted
by the testimony of
that kiss.

NIGHT SONG

*Lying awake
one night,
I was serenaded
by the
first rain of
Spring,
a welcome harbinger
of the departure
of a long
and tedious,
winter.*

The steady splatter
of rain against glass–
like cat claws
tick, tock, ticking
on a tile floor–
a rhythmic
Springtime
sonata.

If it were snow,
the world would become voiceless;
a hush would
stifle nature's ambient rhythms
and obscure them
beneath a cloak
of anonymity.

It's seems
an entire lifetime
has passed
since I've heard the serernade
of sweet
nocturnal music;
an indication of the long-awaited
departure of
winter blues.

ITTY BITTY
KITTY DITTY

*One comment
we often
hear
when people
first encounter
our cats
is:
"They're so big!".*

Our cats are fat.
Can't alter that.
They hiss and moan
at muscle tone!

Each feline meal's
consumed with zeal,
ten times a day
at their buffet.

Food people eat
to them's no treat,
pet fare's just fine
on which to dine.

Then, when inclined,
they'll change their mind,
and seek fresh tastes
to stretch their waists.

To our dismay,
we've found no way
to keep them fit—
And so, we've quit!

SAVANT

Adriana is
a very talented
sculptress.

I am
literal,
and don't
understand
her abstractions
until
she explains
them.

She is a gifted,
honest-to-a-fault,
passionate,
exceedingly
brilliant woman.

Thank you
for conducting me
through
the looking glass.

Your distaff domain,
though
short on
milk and honey
overflows with
concrete, rebar, and
steadfast devotion
to artistic
and moral integrity–
highly essential
to portraying
the
human condition.

96

SNOW

*Looking
at another
snowy day
in Upstate
New York,
can either be
depressing
or
inspirational.*

*The
choice
is ours.*

Powdery pillows
of glittering
gossamer
swirl and pirouette
in synchronized
complicity.

These inundating,
chaste,
pint-sized puffs
deftly dress
the grim tundra
in a dazzling disguise–
temporarily imparting
a look of splendor
to otherwise
seedy
surroundings.

INEVITABILITY

*Too often
we get caught up
in trying to be
what we
are not.*

*Human nature
deceives us
into thinking
the grass is
greener
on the other
side of
the fence.*

*But,
there's
always someone
in the other yard
convinced that
you
are the one
who has
everything.*

No longer captain of my ship,
nor master of my fate,
my ship set sail, put out to sea–
and I arrived too late.

We must act upon our chances,
not dally or demure
for time stands still for no one–
opportunity's insecure.

So, when you see an opening,
if your career bodes you misgiving
take a risk and hasten headlong
towards conditions more forgiving.

We have false expectations
for what we can achieve
and suffer disappointment
when we learn we've been naïve.

The moral of this story–
be sincere in who you are,
don't waste life seeking riches
you may not become a star.

The world is full of people
who decide day-in, day-out
to settle for simplicity,
existence without doubt.

No disgrace in being average,
Not all of us are whizzes.
Untroubled life, that's free from strife
is more pleasant than show-biz is.

OUTCRY

*This is the
age-old
(or old age)
conundrum of
changing
times.*

Why can't I do
what I used to do,
when I used to do
what I wanted to?

Now, compelled to do
what I'm able to
I long for things
that I'd rather do.

RECOGNITION

*We have to
make peace with
who we have
become.*

*We slog
in our own
moccasins,
experience
pain and joy,
and
live and die
on our own.*

*So,
what others
think of us
is not of
any real
consequence.*

Reaching eighty years of age
is a lot like walking the high wire,
with similar concerns:
> *Contemplate each step,*
> *assume nothing,*
> *keep moving,*
> *and don't look down.*

Don't try to entertain the onlookers–
Leave that to daredevils
or foolhardy kids.

You know where you are headed.
You know where you have been.
Since you've survived this long,
you have nothing further to prove.

Now, demonstrate to all those
supercilious young pups,
that you are
> *the quintessential octogenarian*
that they
should aspire to become.

LAMENT

*My dislike
of dying
is primarily
due to the
powerlessness
of disappearing
from
the lives of
people I love.*

*I can't imagine
what it's like
not to exist
or know
what's going on.*

*And, then
there's the dread
of being
forgotten
and
all alone.*

I worry
that I won't be alive
when you say to
your life partner–
"my dad drew this picture",
"wrote this poem",
or "created
this recipe".

I'd swell with pride.

I'd like to
be able to listen to
the tenderness
in your voice,
see the glimmer of affection
in your eyes
that causes you to
blink back tears
as you mention me–

the man who
has loved you intensely
all of your life.

Only in the movies.

ANGELINO

My GP
is the best!
He listens,
reasons,
and
tries his
damnedest
to do
no harm.

Doctor John is quite a doc
He keeps me ticking like a clock,
Sprockets, springs
Click, clack, and ping!
I should be hardy as a king.

Alas, 'taint so.
My gears grind slow
They yammer for repair,
There's crumble, and I'm rusted,
My mainspring's maladjusted.

I don't manage time
As once I did
I understand, I'm not a kid.
Components worn, controls are shot,
A regal presence I am not.

I'm just an aging
Relic of
Impossible, quixotic love
Once part of the madding throng
Now I can see I don't belong.

Though you may try
As best you can,
You can't make me a younger man
I grow decrepit by degrees
My ailments John– *are not disease.*

*A
wonderful gentleman
comes to
the YMCA pool
Tuesday and Thursday
mornings
and we engage in
some really funny
banter.*

*Years ago,
he was a
very active
independent apple farmer,
but now,
he occupies his time
with traveling around
on his electric scooter,
and a friendly game
of poker
every other Tuesday.*

APPLE BOB

He walks a few yards,
leaning heavily on his cane,
and is compelled to pause
to catch his breath,
supporting his back against the wall.
His lungs and energy
will take him no farther.

After a while,
able to breathe easier,
he resumes his trek toward the lobby
where he is obliged once more
to stop for another short rest.
All this, for a cup of coffee
with Art and the fellas.

Often, he questions if this ordeal
is worth the effort.
He can't see the logic for
getting out of bed in the morning,
to be beleaguered by the
huffing and puffing,
and insufferable dizziness.

Eighty-five years is enough!
His precious wife, gone thirty years,
but he still feels lost
without her by his side.

So, when you're eighty-five years old,
only have a thirty percent lung capacity,
and can't abide the struggle of dressing,
you tend to confine your days to
parsimonious activities,
water walking being the one exception.

Is death the only solution? Perhaps.
He's not afraid. Might even welcome it.
But those of us,
whom he brings joyfulness to,
would be impoverished
if deprived of his devilish wit,
and mischievous smile.

PAISAN

*I still can't
wrap my head
around
modern
technology!*

*My son
whips out his
Blackberry
in Italy
and calls home
like he is
just around
the corner.*

Oy!

Joe phoned from Italy today.
Rome.
Standing in Saint Peters Square.
Freakin' amazing!

Just to say hello.
They'd visited the Coliseum.
Now, bound for a tour of The Vatican.
Next, Florence, Venice, and Naples.
He kept saying "Italy is freakin' amazing".

(Pass the potato latkes)

He went to Italy as Jew-boy Joe.
I think he'll come home as Guiseppe!
Freakin' amusing!

*A friend
at the Y
doesn't
realize
she is an
unusual person.*

*She does
what's right
no matter
what others
would have
her do.*

*I wanted her
to know
that she
should relish
another
birthday.*

HAPPY BIRTHDAY RUTH

Unquestionably great
At forty-eight!
You're not defined by age.
What you don't see
And ought agree–
You've merely turned a page.

The book of life
Jam-packed with strife
Is still a stirring read.
Look past your pain
Let me explain
How you're a curious breed.

Where others hedge
Or drive a wedge,
Just criticize and malign,
You don't comment,
Urge they repent
And do something more
Than whine.

SANTA LOSS

It's Xmas eve in Mendon
Jen and Joe are in their beds
We've read the usual stories
Tales of Santa fill their heads.

But first we take a breather
Cause there's lots of work to do
Finish wrapping up the presents
And assembling toys for two.

Their certainty in Santa
Makes deception more worthwhile
There's no delight in Christmas
Without a wide-eyed child.

Grown up, our kids live elsewhere
They absconded with the glow,
And left behind a pointlessness
For a Christmas we don't know.

We used to share sweet holidays,
Then, Christmas was in favor,
Four stockings on the mantlepiece,
Warm hugs we all could savor.

The titter of a young brood's joy
The love, the childhood laughter,
I wish we could relive those days
That's precisely what I'm after.

Now Christmas is like birthdays
Just another check-mark added
None the worse for it, or better,
Doesn't matter if we've had it.

Grandchildren simply aren't the same
They're someone else's line
I crave the joys of yesteryear
When the cuddled kids were mine.

PRUDENCE

*I've matured
and I'm
a lot happier
now.*

*Being right
is not
the be-all
and end-all
that I
once thought
it was.*

As I grew older
I got wise,
I saw things through
my brother's eyes.

Where once inclined
to claim, "I'm right!!"
I forced myself
To stay polite.

Now that I'm mellow
when addressed,
I've become
a welcome guest.

My tongue is curbed
and life's a ball
I live and love
sans vitriol.

SLEIGHT OF HAND

*The Upstate
countryside
is strikingly
beautiful.*

*There is
such a vast
array of
flora here
that adds
dimension
to Fall colors.*

Daylight withers
and declines,
bathing the hillsides
with an opulent
golden orange flush.

The tired landscape
gleams with
iridescent grandeur
that sparkles and shines
as if some
heavenly hand had
seized bits of
the Milky Way
and hurled them down
to blanket
the moldering terrain.

These specks of
cosmic gems
mingle to form
a stunning duvet
that camouflages
the tired panorama–
which has been
at cross-purpose
with the luxurious
patina
of Indian Summer.

AWAKENING

At least
once a year,
I take a
mental health day
to visit my
good friend,
Jack Slutzky.

Jack lives
west of
Rochester, NY
in LeRoy.

The trip
takes me through
suburban areas,
past the prison
at Industry,
onto
back roads
that ramble through
fallow fields
and splendid
panoramic
vistas.

The green-garbed hills
transfix the eye,
a tapestry of texture,
undulating to infinity
defining the bosom, hips, knees
of Mother Earth,
who
doggedly decorates
every crevice, crack,
and chasm,
embroidering the countryside–
revealing nature's
exemplary palette
of peerless hues.

www.ingramcontent.com/pod-product-compliance
Lightning Source LLC
Chambersburg PA
CBHW021343090426
42742CB00008B/728